Disneyland
Secrets

Disneyland Secrets

A Grand Tour of
Disneyland's Hidden Details

Gavin Doyle

Theme Park Press
www.ThemeParkPress.com

Although every precaution has been taken to verify the accuracy of the information contained herein, no responsibility is assumed for any errors or omissions, and no liability is assumed for damages that may result from the use of this information.

Theme Park Press is not associated with the Walt Disney Company.

The views expressed in this book are those of the author and do not necessarily reflect the views of Theme Park Press.

Theme Park Press publishes its books in a variety of print and electronic formats. Some content that appears in one format may not appear in another.

Editor: Bob McLain
Layout: Artisanal Text

ISBN 978-1-941500-42-2
Printed in the United States of America

Theme Park Press | **www.ThemeParkPress.com**
Address queries to bob@themeparkpress.com

This book is dedicated to my parents, Jennifer and Patrick, who instilled in me a sense of whimsy and a belief that anything is possible with determination and hard work. And also to my little sister Charlotte, my best friend and playmate. I am forever thankful for their support and love.

Contents

Introduction

Do you remember the first time you walked under the train tracks and into Disneyland? The first time you saw the castle? Found your first hidden Mickey Mouse? Or heard the Disneyland band for the first time? All of these memories illuminate my childhood like the Disneyland fireworks in the night sky.

My life was changed forever after my first trip to the park as a four year old. Nothing was more magical than the special trips we made to the parks each year. As I grow older, I become even more deeply engrossed in the intricacies of the park and the incredible people that work to create the happiest place on earth.

When I was 13, I started DisneyDose.com and since then I have had the privilege of interviewing some of the most gracious, creative, and fascinating people who work for the Walt Disney Company. I have spent countless hours with Imagineers and Cast Members alike recalling their favorite details and little-known stories and sharing them on our Disney Dose podcast.

Now, after years of reading Disneyland history books, talking with the people who create the park, and searching for details throughout the resort, I am thrilled to present, *Disneyland Secrets*.

Each of the secrets has been verified either through interviews or book sources, which can be found in the bibliography in the back of the book. In seeking to validate each secret that crossed my desk, I eliminated many that lacked historical evidence. Chief Archivist Emeritus of the Walt Disney Archives Dave Smith warned me that absolute verification would be a challenge. Most importantly, he asked that we remember that over time Disneyland Cast Members will make up stories to entertain guests, and as more and more websites report these stories as fact, telling the difference between legend and truth becomes extremely difficult.

All of these details, secrets, and stories come together to help create Walt Disney's original Magic Kingdom and the magic that we all enjoy today. Let's look to the quote by science fiction writer and close friend of Walt Disney, Ray Bradbury. In a letter to Walt Disney (shared by Imagineer Tony Baxter) that Bradbury wrote after first riding the Peter Pan attraction, he sums up the magic of Disneyland saying:

> I shall be eternally grateful that you made it possible for me to fly out of a child's bedroom window in a pirate galleon, setting sail over moonlit London, past the stars and then on to Never-Land.

With this quote fresh in your mind, I invite you to join me on a daring journey through the hidden details and secrets of Disneyland.

Park
Secrets

1

Weeds or Exotic Latin Plants?

On opening day, Disneyland lacked plants and greenery throughout.

Walt Disney had his chief gardeners, Bill and Jack Evans, label the weeds in the flower beds with fancy Latin names on identification cards.

2

Meooowwww

Disneyland is home to between 100–200 feral cats that prowl the grounds.

The cats moved into the park in 1955. To combat the rodent problem, Disney decided to keep the cats around. They set up feeding stations, and spayed and neutered each cat. Cast Members at Circle D Corral keep the cats healthy and happy year round. While the cats mainly stay hidden during the daytime, you are most likely to spot them near their feeding stations in Grizzly Gulch (California Adventure), the Hungry Bear Restaurant (Critter Country), the ivy along the tram path coming from Mickey and Friends Parking Structure, or White Water Snacks in the Grand Californian Hotel.

3

We'll Give You 25 Cents for That Ticket

Guests can exchange old
letter tickets for money.

Many A, B, C, D, and E tickets are
still in circulation around the country. Occasionally, guests will bring
these tickets to Disneyland. Guests
are given the face value of the ticket,
which doesn't amount to very much,
because the most expensive ticket
was only 95 cents. Those trying to get
value out of their tickets would have
better luck selling them on eBay.

4

King Tut, Magician

Steve Martin worked in Disneyland
while he was a teenager.

Martin worked on Main Street selling
programs and eventually graduated into
Merlin's Magic Shop in Fantasyland.
He attributes much of his comedic
timing to practice in the magic shop
and to Disney Legend Wally Boag,
the star of the long-running show,
the Golden Horseshoe Revue.

5

Why 1313?

The address to Disneyland is
1313 Harbor Boulevard.

There are a couple of ideas as to where
this came from. Turned sideways, it
looks like two Mickey Mouse ears.
Or, the thirteenth letter in the alpha-
bet is M. So 1313 represents MM, or
Mickey Mouse. A competing theory
is that the 13 is simply Walt Disney's
lucky number. Seen in other places,
1313 was used as Donald Duck's home
address and 313 was his license plate.

6

Buy Me Some Peanuts

No peanuts or gum are sold in Disneyland.

Anaheim Mayor Charles Pearson didn't want a dirty amusement park in his city. He voiced his concerns to Walt Disney. They both agreed that they would never sell unshelled peanuts or chewing gum inside Disneyland. This rule still holds true today.

7

Don't Look at Me

Many backstage buildings around the resort are painted "no-see-um-green".

Varying hues of green are used based on the surrounding paint. The goal of this "no-see-um-green" is to cause the object to fade into your color spectrum so that your eye will miss it completely. The best example can be found on the outdoor lift hill of Big Thunder Mountain, where you can easily see backstage by turning your head to the right. Most guests simply don't see this backstage area as everything is covered in Disney's special green-colored paint. Other examples include the door into the private Club 33, the show building for Indiana Jones, and the buildings lining the railroad tracks.

8

You Had Better Shave

Originally, Disneyland Cast Members weren't allowed to have facial hair to keep them within the guidelines of the clean Disney Look.

As of 2012, male Cast Members can grow beards, mustaches, and goatees. The Cast Member handbook states that all facial hair must be fully grown in. Perhaps those who started before 2012 and want beards now have to take long vacations to grow them.

9

Coke, No Pepsi

Only Coca-Cola soda products
are sold within Disneyland.

In return for this brand loyalty, Coca-Cola
gives Disneyland free syrup to make all
of the soft drinks. Disney still has to pay
for the containers and cups to serve the
drinks. Pepsi-Cola was an opening day
sponsor of the Golden Horseshoe Revue.
They sponsored the show until 1982.

10

You Won't Drop It

Trash cans are all supposed to be no more than 30 feet apart in Disneyland.

Walt Disney did extensive research at other amusement parks around the country before the construction of Disneyland began. He found that a person would not walk more than 30 steps before dropping a piece of trash.

11

He Called Them What?

The landmarks throughout the parks are called "weenies" as they draw people toward different areas.

According to Disney historian Jim Korkis, Walt Disney would often return home from long days of work at the Studio and in Disneyland and walk into the kitchen. He would grab two hot dogs or "wieners". Using these he found that he could make the family dog, Lady, perform all sorts of tricks and lead her about. Perhaps he referenced this practice to an Imagineer working on Disneyland and the name stuck.

12

Weenie for Lady

The main weenie in the park is Sleeping Beauty Castle, which draws people up Main Street.

Once in the hub, each land has a weenie that is visually enticing: Fantasyland has the King Arthur Carrousel, Tomorrowland has the Astro Orbitor, and Frontierland has the *Mark Twain* and action on the Rivers of America. The only land that doesn't posses a weenie is Adventureland. According to Disney historian Sam Gennawey, if the guests knew too much about this land, it wouldn't be much of an adventure.

13

Split Up the Crowd

Planters are used to control crowds, especially during the busiest times of the year, and create more intimate spaces.

Each of the walkways transversing the parks are designed to maintain a certain capacity. But, for aesthetic reasons, many of these main thoroughfares are split up to avoid large expanses of concrete. Evidence can be seen throughout the park. Examples include the planters throughout the main hub, the multi-tiered esplanade along the Rivers of America, the planters in Tomorrowland, and the planters and benches that divide the walkway in front of the Frontierland Shooting Gallery.

14

"Ladies and Gentlemen, Boys and Girls"

The Disneyland and Disney California Adventure announcers are happily married.

Bill Rogers is the official announcer for Disneyland and announces all shows with his famous line of "Ladies and Gentlemen, Boys and Girls..." Across the esplanade in Disney California Adventure, his wife, Camille Dixon, holds the special position of park announcer.

16

Adventure into Tomorrow

The original position of Adventureland was changed because of existing trees on property.

At first, Tomorrowland and Adventureland would have been on opposite sides of the park. When the huge bank of eucalyptus trees on the left side of Main Street was discovered, the positions of the lands were swapped. These huge eucalyptus trees were planted as windbreaks for the orange groves originally on property.

17

Mickey Mouse Wants You!

All Cast Members, from top executives to street sweeper, go through a training program called Traditions before beginning work.

The program focuses on bringing new hires into the fold and teaching them about the culture and heritage of the Walt Disney Company while featuring the past, present, and future. The goal of the class is to remind every Cast Member that they each play an important role in providing quality and magic to the guests who visit the park. At the conclusion of the ceremony, Mickey Mouse presents each new hire with their official Disneyland name tag.

18

"Hello Mr. Disney... or I Mean, Walt"

Each Disneyland Cast Member name tag features their first name and hometown.

Walt Disney disliked being called Mr. Disney and wanted everyone to just call him Walt. He extended the first name basis requirement to all Disneyland Cast Members by issuing the nametags in 1962. Prior to 1962, each aluminium tag had only the Cast Member's employee number.

19

Now That Is an Increase on Investment

One piece of land across from Disneyland increased in value from $10,000 to $100,000,000.

In 1954, just one year before Disneyland had opened, the Fujishige family purchased 56 acres of strawberry fields across from Disneyland park for $10,000. For years Disney pursued the property. When the Fujishige's finally sold in 1998, 52.5 of the acres sold for $99.9 million dollars. The family still owns 3.5 acres.

20

FAA Requirements Prohibit...

Disneyland and Walt Disney World are some of the only permanent no-fly zones that don't relate to national security.

Disney lobbyists campaigned for no-fly-zones after 9-11. The prohibitions were included in a 2003 budget bill that included Homeland Security measures. The bill was rushed through Congress as tensions were increasing due to the star of the Iraq war. No flight may be within a three-mile radius or below 3,000 feet of Disneyland.

Main Street, U.S.A. Secrets

1

Red Carpet Greets You

The ground when you first enter the park is red brick. Walt Disney wanted it to feel like you were walking in on a red carpet.

Each part of Disneyland was constructed with great thought for the guest experience. In addition to the red brick/red carpet device, the tunnels entering the park are meant to represent the curtains opening on the stage. Once you step through them, you have entered a new world.

2

Lost Parents Sign

There is a "lost parents" sign in front of Disneyland City Hall that reads "Lost Parents Inquire Here for Children".

The parents painted on the sign Mr. and Mrs. Darling whose children left home and joined the Lost Boys in Disney's Peter Pan.

3

City Hall Bookcase

Inside of City Hall there is a bookcase holding fake books with Disney film titles. Mixed in with the real titles is a book that was never written, called *Walt & You*.

The fake book is authored by Sidejas & Kimbrell. Much like the many windows on Main Street that acknowledge key individuals, the author credit is a tribute to Ray Sidejas, the guest services manager for Disneyland Custodial, and Bruce Kimbrell, the business program facilitator for the Disney Institute. Both had an incredible impact on Disneyland and the guest experience, making Guest Services at City Hall the perfect place for their tribute.

4

Cannons in Town Square

These actual cannons were used by the French Army in the 1800s.

Although they were never fired, the French Army owned them during the 1800s. Many public parks around the country contained monuments to the service men of the local town. The Imagineers added these cannons to the Disneyland park to honor the service men of the world.

5

Walt's Window

The lamp in the window of Walt's private apartment above the Disneyland Fire Station was turned on to alert Cast Members that their boss was in the park.

To this day, the lamp is kept constantly lit to remind Cast Members and guests that even though Walt is no longer with us, his vision and creativity still shine on in the world, just like the light of the lamp. The only time that the lamp is touched is when it is switched out for a miniature Christmas tree during the holiday season or, in the past, when Walt Disney's daughters were using the apartment or were present in the park.

6

Test Brick Wall

At the end of a cross street half way up Main Street there is a lonely wall that was built with a combination of different bricks.

The story is that this wall was used to test the various types of bricks and masonry that would be used throughout the park. During the weeks before the opening day of Disneyland, teams were rushed and tight on time. Perhaps the wall was forgotten or simply left as it was built. Either way, the wall has been preserved.

7

Smellitzer

Under the Candy Palace & Candy Kitchen window on Main Street there's a small vent. This vent shoots the fantastic candy smells into the streets.

The Smellitzer was named after the famous WWI shell launcher, the howitzer. Instead of launching deadly shells, it launches glorious aromas.

8

Red & White Lightbulb

An oddly painted lightbulb is part of a string of bulbs at the Coca Cola Refreshment counter at the top of Main Street.

Walt Disney was always a dedicated perfectionist. When he was walking through the park one day, he saw two white bulbs next to each other. They were supposed to alternate from white to red. The problem was that there were an odd number of bulbs outlining the door. To fix the mistake, Walt called one of the painters over and had him paint half of the white bulb red so that the pattern wouldn't be ruined.

9

Disneyland Gas Lamps

The gas lamps that line Main Street are over 200 years old.

The street lamps along Main Street come from Baltimore, Saint Louis, and Philadelphia. They were purchased for only $1 a pound as scrap metal. (I'm sure they would have sold for more if the seller had known that Disney was the buyer.) Originally, a Cast Member lit the lamps each night.

10

Take Me Home, Main Street Road

Walt Disney added Main Street, U.S.A. to the plans with the thought that it would represent his hometown and the hometowns of every American.

Walt's inspiration for Main Street can be traced to his nostalgia for his childhood home of Marceline, Missouri. But the street much more resembles Fort Collins, Colorado, the hometown of Imagineer Harper Goff who designed a majority of the land. Disneyland City Hall is modeled after the Fort Collins County Courthouse.

11

Hop Aboard a Private Car

The Lilly Belle car is a private rail car pulled by the *C.K. Holliday* locomotive., and the last rail car from opening day.

Previously called the Grand Canyon viewing car, it was converted when Disneyland Transportation Supervisor Ken Kohler suggested that the park needed a special car for VIP guests and dignitaries. Walt Disney's wife, Lillian, helped decorate the car, adding family photos and early memorabilia. The car is named the Lilly Belle in her honor. One of the car's first notable guests was Japanese Emperor Hirohito and his wife. Guests can request a ride at the Main Street Train Station. The car is most often available on less crowded days and in the mornings.

13

Wow! That's a Lot of Garland

During the Christmas season,
over one mile of garland is used
to decorate Main Street.

These decorations go up around the
first week of November and are taken
down the first week of January. Until
2008, a real tree from Mount Shasta
graced Main Street every year. In 2008,
the real tree was replaced with a huge
artificial one and is still used today.

14

His Own Private Apartment

Walt Disney maintained a private 500-square-foot apartment above the firehouse on Main Street the entire time that he was alive.

The apartment was complete with a bathroom, living space, tiny kitchen area, and working fire pole. Walt's daughter, Diane Disney Miller, told historian Michael Broggie that one day a small redheaded boy wanted to meet her dad and decided to shimmy up that fire pole for an audience. Walt was in the apartment reading. After multiple such incidents, the hole was boarded up.

15

Irish Vacationer at Smoke Tree

The Partners statue, unveiled in the central hub in 1993, and which portrays Walt Disney holding hands with Mickey Mouse looking out toward the future, has several easily missed references to Walt.

On Walt's tie there is a small insignia for the Smoke Tree Ranch in Palm Springs, CA. Disney had a house there and had the logo stitched into many of his ties. On Walt's right hand there's a Claddagh ring in honor of his Irish heritage. Both Walt and his wife, Lillian, purchased Claddagh rings during their 1948 trip to Ireland and wore them often.

16

Singing or Sawing

The Main Street Opera House was the first building to be completed in 1955.

Until 1961, the Opera House was just a facade for the park's lumber mill during the construction of the park and for the numerous additions made during its first six years. In 1961, the Opera House was converted into the show building for Great Moments with Mr. Lincoln.

17

Dreaming of Disneyland

The park bench where Walt Disney dreamt of Disneyland is preserved inside the front entrance to the Main Street Opera House.

Walt Disney dreamt of Disneyland while sitting on a park bench at Griffith Park, watching his two daughters ride the carousel. It was here that he originally thought of the need for an "amusement enterprise [to be] built, where the parents and the children could have fun together."

18

Why Do I Smell French Fries?

The Disneyland Railroad and the *Mark Twain* riverboat run on the used French fry oil from the restaurants.

Each of the train engines operating on the Disneyland Railroad and *Mark Twain* were converted to burn on a soy-based biofuel. This is just one of the numerous sustainability initiatives throughout The Walt Disney Company.

19

Turn on the Lights

Guest are able to safely exit the park during an electrical power outage because of the light emitted from the gas lamps lining Main Street.

Disneyland experienced a rare complete power outage on December 22, 1982. These gas lamps still come on everyday at dusk.

20

Broken Light Posts Make Good Flagpoles

The base of the Disneyland flag pole is part of a light post from Wilshire Boulevard in Los Angeles.

While driving home, Disney Legend Emile Kuri noticed that one of the light poles had been knocked over in an accident. He purchased the base of the pole on the spot as scrap for $5. The original light pole piece can be identified as the black ornate base.

21

Passing Lane

There is a side track in front of the main Disneyland train station that was built to allow for trains to pass other trains sitting in the station.

When the park opened, there were two trains which only stopped at their own "home station". The freight-themed train only stopped in Frontierland and the passenger train only at Main Street. When park attendance rose, a third train was added. At that point, the "home station" system was scrapped, Fantasyland and Tomorrowland stations were added, and each train stopped at each station.

22

Ridin' Round Town in the Fire Wagon

The fire wagon inside of the Disneyland Fire Station was an opening day attraction.

The wagon was pulled up and down Main Street serving guests until 1960. Horses pulled two other vehicles on opening day: the streetcar and the surrey. The surrey was taken out of commission in 1971, but the streetcar still operates daily.

23

Santa Fe Trains

The original four locomotives on the
Disneyland Railroad were named
for Santa Fe Railroad executives.

The engines were the *C.K.Holliday*, *E.P.
Ripley*, *Ernest S. Marsh*, and *Fred Gurley*.
The Santa Fe company sponsored the
Disneyland Railroad from opening day
until 1974. A fifth engine was added on
June 25, 2005, and is named in honor
of legendary Disney animator and railroad buff Ward Kimball. Coming full
circle, Ward Kimball's grandson Nate
works on the Disneyland railroad and is
often the engineer operating the locomotive named after his grandfather.

24

Wow, It's Chilly in Here

The shops selling clothing through-out the resort are kept a couple of degrees colder to encourage guests to purchase sweatshirts and jackets.

On the opposite end of the spectrum, the pavement of Main Street is black so that it warms up during the day and drives guests off the street and into the shops. Ice cream at Gibson Girl, anyone?

25

Menorah on Main Street

While almost every name stenciled on the windows lining Main Street is real, there is at least one fictitious name.

The window above New Century Jewelry that reads "Dr. Benjamin Silverstein M.D.—General Practitioner—Have a Fever? Have the Flu? —Come on in and We'll Cure You!" was added to provide a fitting place for Hanukkah decorations. A mezuzah can be found outside the door all year long, and a menorah is placed in the upper window during the holiday season.

The mezuzah is traditionally attached to Jewish doorways to fulfill the Biblical commandment to inscribe the words of Shema on the "doorpost" of your home.

26

Clip Clop

Nothing is better than the sounds of Main Street, U.S.A. when the parks open.

One of the most notable sounds is the clopping of the hooves of the horses. The horseshoes have a special polyurethane coating to give them better traction and to increase the clip-clop sound as they walk the streets.

27

Plants and Dishes For All

You can request the name of most plant or any recipe at City Hall.

The landscaping team is responsible for every plant you see in the parks each day. During the no-guests third shift, plants are watered and replaced if damaged. The names of most plants, trees, and flowers are on file at Disneyland City Hall. These records are open to any guest interested. Also available are recipes for many of the dishes prepared throughout the park.

Fantasyland Secrets

1

Snow White's Grotto

The marble statues in Snow White's Grotto were a gift to Walt Disney from Italian sculptor Leonida Parma.

In 1961, huge crates arrived at the Disney Studio with figures from the film *Snow White and the Seven Dwarfs*. The characters had been modeled on soaps that were then being sold in Europe. The problem was that the characters were all the same size, even though Snow White is supposed to be taller than the dwarves. Imagineer John Hench came up with a way to display them using forced perspective to make it appear that Snow White is taller. He created a deer about half Snow White's height and positioned them on a top level above all of the dwarfs.

2

Horse Roundup

All of the horses on King Arthur Carrousel were purchased from other parks.

After being purchased, each of the horses was sanded down and repainted. Disney has a team of painters whose main job is to make sure that all ride vehicles are well-cared for and constantly looking fresh. A main focus of the team is these carrousel horses. There are 70 horses on the carrousel and 13 spares that can be switched out while others are being painted.

3

Cheshire Cat Says Hello

If you look in the large mirror in the Mad Hatter hat shop and wait a few seconds, you'll see the mischievous cat.

This effect is achieved by using a 50% mirror with a light comes on behind it, which lets you see through the mirror itself. The technology is a combination of the special effects used in the Haunted Mansion and the one-way mirror that would be used in an interrogation room.

4

Central Gold Spike

The center spike inside Sleeping Beauty Castle marks the middle of Main Street.

It was placed as a survey marker to make sure that the Castle and train station were both centered on Main Street. There are other gold survey markers throughout the parks that were used for similar purposes.

5

Somebody Stole My Apple!

When the Snow White attraction first opened, the evil queen's apple was constantly taken.

In one scene, the Evil Queen offers riders a red apple. The apple wasn't glued to the figure's hand very tightly and was often stolen by over-zealous guests. Disney solved the problem with mirrors: now, an apple only appears to sit in the Evil Queen's hand now.

6

Jingles the Horse

On the King Arthur Carrousel, one horse is more decorated than the others.

The white horse with the collar that reads "Honorary Ambassador" was dedicated to Julie Andrews for her Disney film work and for her stint as as the official Disneyland ambassador during the 50th Anniversary of the park. The horse is decorated with touches from her most popular film, *Mary Poppins*.

7

Madam in the Yellow Poncho

Mary Blair has a doll dedicated to her inside of "it's a small world".

Blair has long been remembered for her stylized illustrations, use of bright colors, and beautiful design work. Her art is most notably seen in Peter Pan, Alice in Wonderland, and "it's a small world". In 1963, Blair was chosen to lead the team that designed "small world". To honor her work, Walt Disney had a special doll created and added to the attraction. Dancing atop the Eiffel tower, the doll has short cropped hair, blue eyes, and is dressed in a yellow poncho and boots.

8

Just the Bottom

The Matterhorn Bobsleds attraction only uses the bottom ⅔ of the Matterhorn Mountain.

The top ⅓ was unused, until Walt Disney asked the Matterhorn Mountain Climbers what they would like to have in this space that had become their break room. Based upon their request, a basketball hoop was installed and remains there to this day.

9

Back to Front...or Front to Back

The back of Sleeping Beauty Castle was originally supposed to be in the front.

The Castle was modeled after Neuschwanstein Castle in Germany. One day, when Walt Disney Imagineer Herb Ryman was working on details for the model, he placed the top half of the castle on the base backwards. Walt Disney walked in and inspected the model and proclaimed that he liked the castle more than ever. If you look at the back half of the castle that currently faces Fantasyland, it was originally supposed to be the front.

10

Up and Down

Sleeping Beauty Castle has a
real working drawbridge.

The drawbridge has only been operated twice. The first time was in 1955
for the opening day of Disneyland
and the second was after the redesign
of Fantasyland in 1983. New fences
installed in 2014 will prevent future use.

11

Tonight, You Are the Star

When Fantasyland initially opened, the star characters from the films *Peter Pan*, *Snow White*, and *The Adventure's of Ichabod and Mr. Toad* made no appearance in their respective attractions.

The thought was that guests would play the part of the hero in a first-person experience. Almost no one understood this concept, and the characters were eventually added.

12

Get Your Tickets!

When the park opened there were no A, B, C, D, and E tickets.

Each attraction had its own individual ticket booth. The lettered tickets weren't introduced until late 1955. Many of the original individual ticket booths can still be found in Fantasyland. They include the station in front of Casey Jr. Circus Train, the mushroom in front of Alice in Wonderland, the lighthouse in front of the Storybook Canal Boats, and the colorful medieval hut in front of "small world" (this was originally for the carrousel in the middle of Fantasyland).

13

Two Tracks. Your Choice.

The Matterhorn bobsleds have two tracks.

The left track is 30 seconds faster and includes sharper dips and drops. Bob Gurr, the Imagineer behind the attraction, created the designs free hand before the invention of computers. Gurr was also known to be afraid of roller coasters, but mustered the courage to ride some nearby coasters when Walt Disney asked him to do research for the Matterhorn.

14

Tiny Tink

As part of the Fantasy in the Sky fireworks starting June 9, 1961, Tinker Bell flew over the castle for the first time.

The actress playing Tinker Bell was named Tiny Klein. She had worked as a circus performer and burlesque dancer. Klein was 70 years old when she took the part.

15

Tribute to President Wells

Frank Wells is honored inside the Matterhorn with a tribute.

Disney President and Chief Operating Officer Frank Wells passed away in a tragic snow helicopter accident in 1994. He worked for the company from 1984–1994. The supplies that are strewn next to the bobsled tracks are labeled the "Wells Expedition" in honor of his attempt to climb the highest peaks on every continents. Wells also has a dedicated window on Main Street above Disneyana.

16

Swimming Chickens

Pieces of the original Fantasyland Pirate Ship are in Peter Pan's Flight.

From 1955 until 1982, the *Chicken of the Sea* Pirate Ship was one of the main centerpieces of Fantasyland. The large wooden ship served tuna sandwiches, burgers, and hot pies. When Fantasyland was redesigned in 1983 to feature a more permanent storybook feeling, the ship was supposed to be moved over to the "it's a small world" promenade. The poorly made ship had rotted badly after sitting in a small pool of water at the back of Fantasyland for more than 25 years. It became evident that the ship wouldn't be able to be moved, and so pieces of it were salvaged for Peter Pan's Flight.

17

Snow White Castle

Sleeping Beauty Castle was to
be named for Snow White.

But the film *Sleeping Beauty* was in pro-
duction, to be released in 1959, and so the
Castle was named after the princess as
an advertising ploy for the film. In 1957,
once the film's story had been finalized,
a walkthrough attraction was added to
the inside of the castle. The walkthrough
was closed after the 9-11 attacks in 2001,
which caused lower park attendance and
a need for large resort-wide budget cuts.
The walkthrough did not reopen until
2008, with newly designed featuring
a mix of digital and classic touches.

18

Carpe Toad

The coat of arms above the door of Mr. Toad's Wild Ride features the Latin "Toadi Acceleratio Semper Absurda".

This Latin phrase can be translated into a warning of the crazy adventures endured on the attraction and reads, "Speeding with Toad is always absurd".

19

The Great Detective

A famous, non-Disney character is featured inside Mr. Toad's Wild Ride

Behind the middle window of the constabulary is the silhouette of Arthur Conan Doyle's Sherlock Holmes. He can be seen on your upper left just after leaving the pub room.

20

Flying Trees

Trees were originally planted on the roof of "it's a small world" in order to make the large show building appear smaller to match the intimate scale found throughout the rest of Fantasyland.

This technique was stumbled upon by the sculptors in the Model Shop who left trees sitting on the roof of the attraction while planning for construction. Walt liked what he saw, and the rest is history. Today, not many trees remain on top of the show building itself, but rather sit on either side of the attraction.

21

Old White Horses

The King Arthur Carrousel is one of the oldest attractions in the park.

The carrousel was constructed in 1922 for the Sunnyside Beach Park in Toronto. When Disney purchased it, there were an assortment of animals to ride on. But Walt wanted each guest to enjoy a fine galloping horse, so other antique horses were purchased from around the country.

22

Celebrate the Swiss

The coat of arms hanging over the entrance to the Matterhorn represents each of the cantons, or states, of Switzerland.

The large red shield represents the country of Switzerland as a whole. The real life Matterhorn is in the canton of Valais. This is the shield that's half red and half white with thirteen stars.

Tomorrowland Secrets

1

#77 is Following Me

The Space Mountain attraction opened in 1977, which is why that number is everywhere inside of the attraction.

When Space Mountain went under heavy refurbishment before Disneyland's 50th anniversary in 2005, the number 77 was added all along the queue and inside of the attraction in remembrance of the opening year.

2

Large Cosmic Wave Ball Fountain

The fountain consists of a large granite ball and water covering it.

The fountain really is a modern marvel. The huge granite ball weighs over 12,600 lbs. If it were removed from the fountain, a plume of water would shoot 150 feet in the air. That is the amount of water pressure required to make it easy for the ball to roll and move when pushed lightly by guests.

3

Route 55

On Autopia there are many different signs honoring Disneyland's past.

The sign "Route 55" honors the year 1955 when Disneyland opened. Inside of the Car Park section is one of the original Mr. Toad's Wild Ride cars that was bronzed and a car from the original midget Autopia, the extra-small version of Autopia that was in Fantasyland from 1956–1965. The midget Autopia was given to Walt Disney's hometown of Marceline, Missouri, after it was removed from the park in 1966. The ride operated in the town for a couple of years, but was soon closed due to expense and the fact that Walt Disney couldn't ride it.

4

"It's a Trap!"

There's a real movie prop inside Star Tours: the Adventures Continue.

The C-3PO Audio-Animatronics figure that greets guests at the front of the Star Tours queue is a real costume worn by Anthony Daniels from the *Star Wars* films. The costume was outfitted by Walt Disney Imagineering to be turned into an Audio-Animatronics figure. The C-3PO costume is plated in gold leaf to give it that shiny look and to avoid oxidation while filming in the desert.

5

Made in Glendale

The queue of Buzz Lightyear Astro Blasters is lined with big battery boxes.

Many of these props are labeled Glendale, California, USA. The batteries pay tribute to the home of Walt Disney Imagineering, the creative team of people behind everything in the Disney parks.

6

Yum

Each plant in Tomorrowland is edible.

Imagineers added edible plants to Tomorrowland during the 1998 retheme to "Imagination and Beyond". To this day, all of the plants are supposed to still be edible, supporting the concept of sustainability, but I'm not sure if I would test this Disneyland secret.

7

Came in Like a Wrecking Ball

Monsanto's House of the Future was one of Tomorrowland's original attractions opening in 1957.

This all-plastic house contained every convenience from the future, including microwaves and other Jetson-type inventions. When the house was removed in 1967, what was originally supposed to be a one-day demolition took two weeks. The wrecking ball continually bounced off of the huge plastic house, and hacksaws were eventually needed. The crews were unable to fully remove the foundation of the house. One corner remains and has been painted green to blend in with the plants near the entrance to the Pixie Hollow meet and greet.

8

Here Comes the Comet

Main Street and Tomorrowland
were both originally meant to represent two Halley's Comet years.

The original Tomorrowland was meant
to represent the year 1986. This was
considered to be a milestone year
that was far in the future, during
the construction of the land in 1955.
Coincidentally, Main Street, U.S.A. also
represents a Halley's Comet year, 1910.

9

Just Put Them Back on the Track

The check-out counter in Store Command is made up of two old PeopleMover cars.

The PeopleMover track still lays dormant in Tomorrowland, and hasn't been used since the failed Rocket Rods attraction was removed in 2001. Other old cars from the PeopleMover are used as picnic tables at Walt Disney Imagineering headquarters in Glendale.

10

Find the Microscope

There is a tribute to Adventures Thru Inner Space inside Star Tours.

Prior to housing the Star Tours attraction, the building was home to Adventure Thru Inner Space. As part of the new Star Tours 2.0, a tribute to Adventures Thru Inner Space was added. In the Death Star scene during your flight, look to the left and you can spot the mighty microscope from Adventures Thru Inner Space.

11

Stripped Geese

Two of the geese from America Sings
are now naked inside Star Tours.

The Audio-Animatronics from America
Sings were repurposed into other attractions. The majority of the singing critters
were transplanted in Splash Mountain,
but a few remained in Tomorrowland,
where they took up residence in Star
Tours. Two of the geese were stripped of
their feathers and became the G2 repair
droids in the original version of Star
Tours. In Star Tours 2.0, the geese were
cleaned up and now run the scanner that
all guests pass through as they board
the ride. If you take a look at their feet,
you can see that they remain webbed.

12

Jetting into a Store Near You

Some of the display cases inside of the Little Green Men Store Command are reused rocket ships from the original Rocket Jets Tomorrowland attraction.

These rocket ships are turned on their sides and have been gutted, with the seats replaced by shelves.

13

Disney, Commander-in-Chief

The original Disneyland Submarine Voyage was comprised of eight submarines.

Based on world rankings at the time, this made Walt Disney the commander of the eighth largest submarine fleet in the world.

14

Dinosaurs in the Future

The planters outside Space Mountain adjacent to Pizza Port contain large "dinosaur" eggs.

While nothing has ever been confirmed, many believe that these eggs are supposed to be dinosaur eggs. This is either an indication that there will be dinosaurs in the future, or these are the eggs from the dinosaurs in the nearby Primeval World display seen while aboard the Disneyland Railroad.

Adventureland Secrets

1

In the Tiki, Tiki, Tiki Restaurant?

Originally, the Tiki Room was designed as a restaurant. Only later was it turned into a show.

The Tiki Room is one of two attractions in Disneyland that has a dedicated restroom. Not only is it a cool secret, but also a great thing to know when there is a long line at the main Adventureland restroom just across the path.

2

Indiana Jones' Feet Hurt

After that long of a walk you
might need a secret bathroom.

If you wait to ride Indiana Jones
Adventure in the regular queue, you could
walk more than half a mile. When the
attraction first opened, the wait time was
ALWAYS over three hours long. People
had to go to the bathroom so badly by
the time that they got to the front of the
line that often they would have to leave
before riding the attraction to find a
restroom. So a restroom was built out of
necessity. This is one of the two attractions that has a dedicated restroom.

3

Just Another Truck. But Wait...

A cargo truck is parked in front of the Indiana Jones Adventure.

The truck is a real prop from the filming of *Raiders of the Lost Ark*. The license number, missing hood ornament, and build are all an exact match. The bars protruding from the front bumper of the truck are meant to assist stunt men climbing on the truck while filming. The bars have golf balls mounted on the top for a better grip. An ore car from the second Indiana Jones film can also be found in the queue.

4

I'm Just Eeyore

Inside of the Indiana Jones Adventure in the safety video room ask a Cast Member to see Eeyore.

Hidden behind the projector there is a sign from the Eeyore parking lot that is very hard to see unless you have a flash light. The sign is here because the Indiana Jones Adventure was built on the site of the old Winnie the Pooh parking lot.

5

My Friend Bones

While riding Indiana Jones Adventure, you may catch sight of a skeleton wearing a pair of Mickey Mouse ears.

The Disney Cast Members who clean Indiana Jones Adventure get to have a special fun of their own. They named one of the skeletons inside the attraction "Bones". About half the time the skeleton is sporting a pair of embroidered Mickey Mouse ears with "Bones" written across the front.

6

Don't Get This Song Stuck in Your Head!

"Swisskapolka", the theme song from the original Swiss Family Robinson Treehouse attraction, still plays on a phonograph in the upper room of the treehouse.

Many have joked that the theme of the treehouse was switched from Swiss Family Treehouse to Tarzan's Treehouse because the song was way too catchy.

7

Jungle Cruise Schematics

In the queue, schematic drawings of Jungle Cruise boats hang on the wall.

These concept sketches were the actual designs for the original Jungle Cruise boats as developed by Walt Disney Imagineering (WED). Each schematic includes the name of Imagineer Harper Goff and an official stamp of approval from WED at the bottom.

8

Jungle King...Lion Cruise

At the tribal scene of the Jungle Cruise, one of the shields displays the logo for *The Lion King* (musical).

The musical version of *The Lion King* is the most successful musical ever and has played for millions of people around the world. This shield can be tough to spot, but if you look hard enough you can find it resting against a tent behind the tribesmen.

9

Live Gators!

When the Jungle Cruise originally opened, live alligators were kept in pens near the queue to entertain guests.

The problem was that many guests believed these animals were fake, just like the animals on the ride, and threw popcorn at the animals to test their theory. Occasionally, the gators would get out of their cages and escape into the Jungle Cruise lagoon. Trainers would have to be called from the nearby Buena Park Gator Farm to retrieve the animals.

10

Roooarrrr!

Sabor the leopard has something to say in the Tarzan Treehouse.

If you lean in toward the scene that feaures Sabor, a huge blast of air will hit you in the face along with an incredible roar. The Swiss Family Robinson tree house was transformed into the Tarzan Treehouse in 1999 in order to make the attraction more relevant for young audiences and to save the treehouse from being taken out completely.

11

"Turn that Tree Around"

Some of the orange and walnut trees populating the riverbanks of the Jungle Cruise were intentionally planted upside down to make them look more exotic.

The hope was that their roots would twist and spread, creating a top layer for the jungle.

12

Get Your Hands (I Mean Feet) Dirty

The final plans for the Jungle Cruise were made on the Disneyland construction site, by Imagineer Harper Goff.

He used a sandbox to sculpt the sand into the shapes of the jungle river. Once completed, the bulldozers replicated his sandy forms.

13

Sounds of Adventure

Indiana Jones had a Disneyland connection before the attraction was even in planning.

While working on the second film, Steven Spielberg sent sound designers to record the sounds of the Big Thunder Mountain Railroad for use in the huge mine car chase scene. These sounds were actually not made by the roller coaster, but created by the Disney Imagineers by recording real locomotives and speeding up the result.

14

Disney Latin

The tree holding Tarzan's Treehouse has been classified by into a special category of Disney species.

The Latin category name is *Disneyodendron Semperflorens Grandis*, or large ever-blooming Disney tree. The original tree was modeled after a large Moreton Bay Fig that still stands in Anaheim less than two miles north of the park.

15

Oldest Tree

The large palm tree located between the queues for the Jungle Cruise and Indiana Jones is the oldest living thing on Disneyland property.

The tree was planted in 1896. When Disney purchased the land, the owners (the Dominguez family) requested that the tree be saved. The original Disneyland landscaping team transplanted it into the current location. Originally, the tree was planted in the area slated for Parking Lot C, but the entire Jungle Cruise queue building was redesigned around the tree.

16

Tiki Masks to the Stars

An outside group called Oceanic Arts designed the Tiki masks lining the fence dividing the Tiki Room courtyard and the main path through Adventureland.

This firm has helped to design countless other Tiki installations for restaurants, theme parks, and movie props. Most notably, they built the Vietnamese village in Forrest Gump and the thatched roof of the hut on the *Gilligan's Island* TV show. They also provided all of the decor for the Polynesian Village Resort in Walt Disney World and the giant totem pole in the Canada Pavillion at Epcot.

17

Watch Out for That Hippo

The guns carried by the skippers on the Jungle Cruise can fire two types of ammo.

The "show ammo" is the quieter sound that they fire in the hippo scene. The second ammo is the "breakdown ammo" which is fired in case of emergency. Three shots indicate some mechanical problem, and four shots are sent off in cases of medical or security dangers. In this case, all of the boats will speed back to the dock to be evacuated, leaving a clear path for the boat that sent out the distress call to return to the dock.

Frontierland
Secrets

1

Mike Fink's Keel Boats

Guests aboard the *Mark Twain* riverboat will see an abandoned house boat along the shore.

Mike Fink, of the *Davy Crockett* series, had a keel boat named the *Gullywhumper* which now sits moored on the banks of the Rivers of America. The boat is a tribute to the television series, the full-length feature films, and the Mike Fink Keel Boats attraction that circled the Rivers of America from 1955–1997.

2

Petrified Tree

A petrified tree is located in front
of the Golden Horseshoe Revue.
The stump was just too big for
Mrs. Disney's home garden.

In 1956, Walt Disney purchased a petrified tree stump from a tree that once
stood 200 feet tall in the Pike Forest
Fossil Beds in Colorado. The tree stump
was sent to California. Walt presented
it to his wife, Lillian, for their 31st
wedding anniversary. Unsure what to
do with the large tree stump, Lillian
donated the tree to Disneyland in 1957.

3

Pardoned Turkeys in Disneyland

From 2005 to 2010, the two turkeys that were pardoned by the President at the White House each Thanksgiving were sent to either Disneyland or Walt Disney World.

The practice was abandoned because of the difficulty and space required to house these large turkeys. One of the pardoned turkeys still remains at Disneyland, but will spend the rest of his time backstage because he can be unruly around guests. Now, presidentially pardoned turkeys are sent to Mount Vernon, George Washington's estate in Virginia.

4

Joe's Ditch

Disney Legend Admiral Joe Fowler was the head supervisor of all West Coast shipyards during WWII. Fowler served in both world wars and retired from the U.S. Navy in 1948. Walt Disney hired him to direct the construction of the *Mark Twain* riverboat and the Rivers of America area. Fowler believed that a dry dock harbor area was necessary for the operation of the ships, but Walt thought it was a waste of space and money.

The space was called Joe's Ditch until the first time that repairs were necessary for the ships. Then Walt realized its usefulness and it was renamed Fowler's Harbor. Joe Fowler went on to direct the construction of Walt Disney World.

5

Floating Down the River

Real logs were used to build the
fort on Tom Sawyer's Island.

To transport these full-sized tree logs to
the island, they were floated across the
river similar to the way that logs were
transported in old-fashioned wood mills.

6

Frontierland Train Station

The Frontierland Train Station was a replica of a movie prop that features a speech in Morse code.

The station was built as a copy of the set for the film *So Dear to My Heart*. It originally sat on the park side of the railroad tracks, but it was moved when the trains began to stop at each station. Walt Disney's Disneyland dedication speech is played in Morse code from the station across the tracks. With the construction of New Orleans Square, the station was renamed for the new area.

7

President or Pow-Wow-er

The Abraham Lincoln Audio-Animatronics figure, used in the Great Moments with Mr. Lincoln attraction until 2005, is now the shaman in the Indian village alongside the Rivers of America.

The figure is draped in shawls and has his face covered. The character uses the same movements originally programed for Lincoln's speech in Great Moments.

8

Mutiny on the *Columbia*

The design of the Sailing Ship *Columbia* is based upon the plans of the HMS *Bounty* because no plans or photos could be found of the original *Columbia*.

The *Bounty* was the setting for one of the greatest mutiny stories in history. Just off the coast of Tahiti, Captain William Bligh was put out in a small boat with 18 of the crew members that were loyal to him. Bligh successfully made it back to England, reported the mutiny, and ships were sent out to capture the mutineers. Architect Ray Wallace used the *Bounty* plans to design the *Columbia*.

9

There Be Silver in De Masts

The construction crew placed a silver dollar under each mast of the Sailing Ship *Columbia* in accordance with the maritime tradition of mast stepping.

This tradition can be traced back to the Roman custom of placing coins in the mouths of men fallen on the battlefield to pay Charon for ferrying their bodies across the River Styx into the underworld. Early sea travel was so dangerous that coins were placed in the masts to ensure a safe crossing into the underworld, should a ship sink. This tradition is still practiced by the US Navy. Sadly, the Disneyland coins went missing after the *Columbia's* wooden masts were replaced with steel masts in the early 1990s.

10

Water-Be-Gone

When they first filled the Rivers of America with water, the construction crews returned the next day to find the river dry because of the absorbent soil.

The river was then lined with clay and refilled. Thankfully, the water didn't go anywhere this time.

11

Up or Down?

On Big Thunder Mountain, there are two special horseshoes in the attraction.

Just before entering the first tunnel there is a horseshoe with the open side facing up, which symbolizes keeping the luck inside. Then, before entering the final mine shaft, you pass a "Keep Out" sign and a horseshoe with the open side facing down, which lets the luck out and might explain why the cavern is caving in.

12

Go Fish

During the early years of Tom Sawyer's Island, guests could go fishing in a regularly stocked pen.

The park provided poles, hooks, and bait to catch the stocked catfish. After many fish carcasses were found stashed throughout the parks, the attraction was closed for good.

13

A Boom or a "Laod Bhang"

A sign in Frontierland for "Laod Bhang and Co" promotes the nightly fireworks, but also cheekily reminds guests of the incredible noise.

Even though the original *Disneyland* television show introduction features the Disneyland fireworks, they didn't debut until 1956. The fireworks were brainstormed as a way to keep guests in the parks eating dinner and staying longer.

14

Fantastical Peaks of Frontierland

Disneyland's Big Thunder Mountain Railroad is based upon the peaks of Utah's Bryce Canyon National Park, while the counterpart in Walt Disney World is based on Monument Valley.

Imagineer Tony Baxter chose the Bryce Canyon Mountain Range as inspiration for the Disneyland version because of the fantastical imaginative colors and shape of the peaks. At Disneyland, the mountain is visible from some parts of Fantasyland, while the Disney World attraction can only be seen from the Frontierland area.

15

Walking Through Nature's Wonderland

Many pieces of the Mine Train Through Nature's Wonderland are still in Frontierland.

The Rainbow Ridge mining town was relocated to the end of Big Thunder Mountain. The open train tunnel that dead ends across the path from Big Thunder Mountain used to carry the train out to the edge of the Rivers of America. There are still jumping fish props from the original attraction in the pond in front of the tunnel. The last remaining locomotive from Mine Train sat on these tracks along the river until 2010, when it was removed for refurbishment to the Carolwood Pacific Historical Society.

16

Real Equipment in Dem Der Hills

A majority of the mining equipment throughout the queue and attraction of Big Thunder Mountain is authentic.

Imagineers searched swap meets, abandoned mines, and ghosts towns throughout Wyoming, Nevada, Colorado, and Minnesota to find enough authentic equipment.

17

Selling Smokes in Disneyland

Main Street and Frontierland each opened with a Disneyland Tobacco Shop selling cigarettes, tobacco, and cigars. Both shops even had complimentary Disneyland match books.

The old Main Street shop is now home to the 20th Century Music Company, while the Frontierland location is the pin shop next door to the shooting gallery. The Indian that signified the tobacco shop can still be found in front of the music store and pin shop.

18

Hop Aboard the *Mark Twain*!

There are three deck levels on the *Mark Twain* Riverboat: the main, promenade, and Texas decks. The wheelhouse is above them.

The top (Texas) deck is open to guests. It was named for the view seen from early ships that sailed the Rio Grande River. From this top deck, passengers could see the northern Texas bank of the river.

19

Audio-Animatronics Burial

Guests who stand on the Big Thunder trail adjacent to the open train tunnel will find themselves directly above a massive Audio-Animatronics resting place.

Some of the old characters from Mine Train Through Nature's Wonderland were buried under the cement being poured for the creation of Big Thunder Mountain. Characters from the attraction were also moved to the Walt Disney World Big Thunder Mountain.

20

Where Walt Sat

Walt Disney had a private box in the Golden Horseshoe that was reserved whenever he was in the park.

Today, the box can be identified as the side box at stage level. Walt's brother Roy often attended the show as well, but usually opted for a front-row table. The Golden Horseshoe Revue set a Guinness World Record for greatest number of theatrical performances when they completed their $42,921^{st}$ show. The show took its curtain call for the last time in 1986.

New Orleans Square Secrets

1

Disney Initials

The initials of both Walt and Roy Disney are carved into the railings of the deck above the Pirates of the Caribbean attraction.

Their initials are hidden in the decorative railing on the Disney Dream Suite's front deck. This would have been the front patio of the planned Disney family apartment in New Orleans Square.

2

What Is 1764?

There is a bricked-up sunken archway in the esplanade along the riverfront, in front of the Haunted Mansion. The archway is labeled 1764.

This small crypt entrance was added sometime around 1990 as a reminder of the long forgotten goal to create a story linking Pirates of the Caribbean, the Haunted Mansion, and Tom Sawyer's Island. There is a lot of mystery surrounding the proposed story, but it centers on a real pirate from the early 1800s named Jean Laffite. As for "1764", it reportedly comes from subtracting 200 years from the birth date of an Imagineer who worked on the project.

3

Lego Captain Jack Sparrow

Hidden in the treasure room of the Pirates of the Caribbean attraction is a Lego Captain Jack Sparrow.

This Lego figure was probably added during the 2006 refurbishment when all of the props from the films were added and the story line was changed.

4

Haunted Mansion Pet Cemetery

A hidden pet cemetery exists on the grounds of the Haunted Mansion.

The cemetery was added to the Haunted Mansion in the 1980s. It's rarely seen by guests, except for those using the handicapped ramp or people who specifically request to see the cemetery. Each morning, Cast Members will find gravestones pushed over. No one knows if this is the work of the playful pet spirits or the Disneyland ducks that occasionally sleep there.

5

Spiderweb Hole

A large spider web festoons the ball-room in the Haunted Mansion.

This web was added when a guest with a slingshot made a hole in the large glass panels that separate the hallway from the ballroom. The glass is built into the foundation of the Haunted Mansion and so it would be very costly to remove.

6

From 20,000 Leagues to 999 Ghosts

The organ in the ballroom scene of Haunted Mansion is an original prop from the film *20,000 Leagues Under the Sea*.

The prop was first used in Disneyland for an exhibit about the film that opened in 1955. After the short-lived exhibit closed, the organ was taken to prop storage. When the prop was added to the Haunted Mansion, all of the pipes and designs were rebuilt, but the original base, keys, and buttons remain.

7

Whose Was It?

Inside the Pirates of the Caribbean there is a real skull on the headboard.

When the attraction first opened, all of the skeleton heads were real. They were purchased from the UCLA Medical Center. The only remaining real skeleton can be found in the treasure room on the headboard of the bed.

8

Well, Are You Dead or Not?

Many of the Haunted Mansion tomb-stones represent real Walt Disney Imagineers who worked on the attraction.

Some of the names are reordered into word jumbles. For example, Art Director Fred Joerger is F. Regreoj, and first female Imagineer Harriet Burns is H. Snrub.

9

Boo!

During the mid-1980s, Cast Members were stationed throughout the Haunted Mansion hallways to scare guests.

These costumed Cast Members were dressed in suits of armor and popped out at guests in the hallway scene. They helped to make the attraction much scarier. The knight was removed due to budget cuts in the character department, guests attacking the character, and a decreased hourly capacity for the attraction due to the shut-offs caused each time a guest hit the knight.

10

Wake Up, Then Dream

Pirates of the Caribbean is designed to be a reverse dream sequence.

The opening bayou scene represents modern day. Inside the caverns, in the dead drunken skeleton room, there is a portrait of a red-headed female pirate. This is a picture of the redhead from later in the attraction long after she has acclimated herself to the pirate lifestyle. The Disneyland Paris attraction is laid out in a different order, beginning with the scenes of live pirates and ending in the skeleton room. This reversal is intended to preach the message that gold and greed will lead to certain death.

11

Apartment Number 2

A second apartment was planned for the Disney family above Pirates of the Caribbean in New Orleans Square.

Walt Disney passed away before the completion of the area in 1967. The proposed apartment was instead built as offices before being converted into the high-end Disney Gallery. In 2008, the gallery was converted into the Disney Dream Suite and is used today by contest winners, Make a Wish kids, and Disney executives. The newly decorated Dream Suite copies the original plans for Walt Disney's apartment, but adds some 21st century touches.

12

Pirate Ghosts

The ship weathervane is from a different version of the Haunted Mansion.

Originally, the Haunted Mansion was to be called "Bloodmere Manor" and revolve around the story of a sea captain and his bride. The exterior of the mansion was completed many years before the final version of the attraction, so the weathervane is in the shape of a ship in keeping with the original plot line.

13

The Mayor of New Orleans or New Orleans Square?

The two New Orleans mayors have had notable interactions with Disneyland.

The mayor of New Orleans in 1966, Victor H. Schiro, was on hand for the dedication of New Orleans Square. He told Walt that the area really did resemble his city. Walt joked back: "But it's cleaner." Schiro was officially made the mayor of New Orleans Square. In 2006 Kimberly Butler, a mayoral candidate for New Orleans, also visited New Orleans Square—at least in Photoshop form. Butler's campaign used a Photoshopped image of her in front of New Orleans Square. Once the media got wind of it, the photo was removed from her website. Butler lost the election.

14

Original Concept Aaaarrrrrt

There is original Disneyland concept art inside the pirate game in New Orleans Square.

During the first years that Pirates of the Caribbean operated, there was a pirate-themed arcade at the exit. One of the games remains in the breezeway between the Pieces of Eight store and Le Bat en Rouge shop. The pirate map inside the game is original concept art for the Pirates of the Caribbean attraction drawn by Disney artist Sam McKim. McKim is best known for his souvenir Disneyland maps.

15

"They're All Staring at Us!"

When walking from the stretching room to your Doom Buggy inside the Haunted Mansion, two busts continue to stare at you.

This effect was discovered by designers Rolly Crump and Yale Gracey who were working on the head for the Abraham Lincoln Audio-Animatronics figure. The rubber mold for the presidential figure was somehow turned inside out. They realized that the eyes of the mold would follow them. This accidental discovery became the basis for the two busts that will never stop staring you down.

16

Thanks, Mary

The box office success of *Mary Poppins* helped to fund many projects at the Disney Studio and Disneyland.

This money was not only used to build New Orleans Square and Pirates of the Caribbean, but helped to create the entire Audio-Animatronics manufacturing arm of Walt Disney Imagineering (WDI). The small sparrow that sings in "A Spoonful of Sugar" was developed by WDI. This division of WDI is called MAPO today in honor of the film.

17

No, Don't Spray Those with Water

The flames in the Pirates of the Caribbean look so real that the Anaheim Fire Department was concerned they would not be able to tell the difference between the real and faux flames during an emergency.

Even though they realized that it was all part of the show, a special system was put in place to shut off the burning town effect in the case of an actual fire.

18

Consider This
Disquieting Metamorphosis

The auctioneer in the Pirates of the Caribbean is voiced by Paul Frees, who also voices the "dead men tell no tales" narrator of the attraction.

Frees is most famously known as the ghost host in the Haunted Mansion and previously voiced Ludwig Von Drake when he hosted the *Wonderful World of Disney* TV show.

19

Hoist the Sails and Make Way

High above New Orleans Square there is the mast of an old sailing ship.

The mast is supposed to be part of a ship sitting in a lake that is on one side of the city of New Orleans. Imagineers based the location on actual geography. This ship was originally planned for New Orleans Square by Disney Imagineer Herb Ryman, who created the concept art for the area, but the sails were cut from the budget. The ship and the sails were finally added during the 1990s. In addition, the mast helps to hide the Disneyland Hotel towers, which is one of the reasons that New Orleans Square was built in the first place.

Critter Country Secrets

1

Max, Buff, and Melvin

The three head fixtures from the Country Bear Jamboree are all inside the Many Adventures of Winnie the Pooh.

The classic characters Melvin the Moose, Buff the Buffalo, and Max the Moose from the Country Bear Jamboree are all still present inside Disneyland at the Many Adventures of Winnie the Pooh. To see them, you have to wait until you're in the room following the Heffalumps and Woozles Honey Room, and then turn around and look at the wall behind you.

2

Mr. Bluebird

Mr. Bluebird from the "Zip-a-De-Do-Dah" theme song of Splash Mountain can be found throughout Critter Country.

Against the wall of the Critter Country store is the house of Mr. Bluebird. He can also be found sitting on a branch waving to guests inside the final scene of Splash Mountain after the 15-story drop.

3

Mermaids in the Mountain

The name of Splash Mountain came about due to the success of the film *Splash*.

When Disney CEO Michael Eisner saw the Tom Hanks film *Splash*, he ordered something from the film to be added to the new water ride. The movie was about a mermaid in Manhattan and didn't have anything to do with the cute characters from *Song of the South*, the film upon whch the ride is based. One Imagineer jokingly said that we could call it "Splash Mountain". The name stuck, and it was used instead of the original name of Zip-A-Dee-Doo-Dah River Run.

4

Most Audio-Animatronics

Splash Mountain is home to the most Audio-Animatronics, clocking in at 103.

While some of them were custom designed for the attraction, many were brought over from the Tomorrowland attraction, America Sings. Characters from America Sings were repurposed here and in the Star Tours queue. The repurposed figures can be seen mainly in the finale scene after the final drop.

5

Little House on the River

The Briar Patch store is the only original structure that remains in Critter Country.

When the small log cabin store first opened in 1956, it was the Indian Trading Post, selling handmade jewelry and goods to complement the authentic Native American performances nearby. When the entire land was gutted and turned into Bear Country in 1972, the store remained. With the addition of Splash Mountain in 1989, the store became the Briar Patch.

Toontown Secrets

1

Dog Barking Out the Fire Window

A guest who presses the doorbell at the firehouse will hear a Dalmation barking out of the window above.

This dog is believed to be one of the canines from *101 Dalmatians*.

2

WDI Trees

Three trees along the backdrop of Toontown behind Minnie's house form the letters WDI.

WDI stands for Walt Disney Imagineering. They are the team of designers who create everything that is included in the Disney theme parks around the world.

3

Jack-o-Lindquist

There is a pumpkin in Goofy's garden designed to look like Jack Lindquist, the first president of Disneyland, complete with a replica of Lindquist's glasses.

This homage to Jack was just his style, but he has been quoted saying that he will never love it as much as his window on Main Street, U.S.A. above City Hall. The window reads: "J.B. Lindquist, Honorary Mayor of Disneyland, Jack of All Trades, Master of Fun."

4

Boomb, Hello, and Poof

There are many gags around Toontown that you shouldn't miss.

- When drinking from the water fountains, they'll talk back and make cracks such as "Leave Some for the Ocean".

- Stand on the manhole cover in the middle of the street and it will talk back to you.

- Every hour the Mickey Mouse clock in the center of the land will put on a short show.

- Pulling on the door marked "Do Not Pull" will cause Roger Rabbit to be electrocuted.

5

An International Mouse

Mickey Mouse's passport can be found in a glass case in his house in Toontown.

The book is stamped with the names of the five locations of Disney parks around the world. They are Anaheim, Orlando, Hong Kong, Paris, and Tokyo. Each is dated with their opening day. No stamp has yet been added for the opening of Shanghai Disneyland.

6

Roof Is a No Go

Originally, the Who Framed Roger Rabbit? attraction was going to feature a trip along the rooftops of Toontown. The idea was scrapped because of the amount of upward climbing track that would have been required to get the cars to the roof and back down.

But, strong enough steel and wide enough pathways to support the ride vehicles had already been added to the second story of the buildings surrounding the attraction. This upper balcony-like area can still be seen in front of the Gag Warehouse building. The Tokyo Disneyland Toontown was replicated exactly, even adding an identical balcony sturdy enough to handle vehicles which is still unused.

Share This Book

Congratulations, you have finished the book—or maybe you just jumped to the final page. Either way, you have arrived.

We would like to thank you for purchasing the book. I have written additional bonus material that includes more secrets, scavenger hunts, and every digital file version of the book. Go to DisneyDose.com/book and enter code DSBYGD and your email; we will send you all of the bonuses. Thank you again for purchasing.

For more information and even longer back stories for many of these secrets, listen to the Disney Dose podcast. Each one of our episodes starts off with a Disneyland Secret. Find the podcast at DisneyDose. com/ddpodcast.

Want to a free limited edition Disneyland Secrets t-shirt? Take a photo of yourself holding the book or reading the book or displaying the book in some creative way, and then post the photo on either Instagram or Twitter using the hashtag #disneylandsecretsbook. On Instagram tag us @DisneylandSecretsBook and on Twitter tag us @DisneyDose.

Every week we will pick the best photo. That reader will win an exclusive limited edition t-shirt featuring the cover art of the *Disneyland Secrets* book.

So, what are you waiting for? Snap that picture and win your t-shirt.

Acknowledgments

I am thankful for the following people who helped to make this book a reality:

To Jennifer Doyle, my mom, who listened to every idea and proofread every word. Neither the book nor website would be possible without her unwavering support in everything that I do. Thank you for always being there.

To Sam Gennawey, author of *Walt Disney and the Promise of Progress City*, *The Disneyland Story*, and *Universal Versus Disney*, for the fantastic insight into the history of Disneyland and the hours he took reviewing multiple drafts of the book.

To Dave Smith, Chief Archivist Emeritus for the Walt Disney Company, for the stories he has shared and kindness he has spread.

To Bob McLain, my incredible Theme Park Press publisher, who believed in the idea of the book and supported me all along the journey. Thank you for the marvelous work you have done.

To the hundreds of Disney Cast Members and Walt Disney Imagineers whom I have interviewed over the last couple of years both for the Disney Dose podcast and in the parks. This book is built on your stories. Thank you for the magic you bring to our lives each and every day.

Bibliography

Broggie, Michael. *Disney's Railroad Story*. Pentrex, 1998.

Flores, Russell. *Seen, Unseen Disneyland*. Synergy Books Publishing, 2012.

Gennawey, Sam. *The Disneyland Story*. Keen Communications, 2014.

Hoffman, David. *Little-Known Facts About Well-Known Places: Disneyland*. Fall Rivers Press, 2008.

Imagineers, The. *Walt Disney Imagineering: A Behind the Dreams Look at Making the Magic Real*. Hyperion Press, 1996.

Koenig, David. *Mouse Tales*. Bonaventure Press, 1994.

Lindquist, Jack. *In Service to the Mouse*. Neverland Media and Chapman Press, 2010.

Strodder, Chris. *The Disneyland Encyclopedia*. Santa Monica Press, 2012.

Wright, Alex and The Imagineers. *The Imagineering Field Guide to Disneyland*. Disney Editions, 2008.

Various Interviews both on the Disney Dose podcast and in person.

About the Author

Gavin Doyle has been a Disneyland enthusiast since his first visit at age four. His first memory is of a rainy day where the park was joyously empty. The bliss of walking onto any ride with no line fed his initial love for Disneyland. He continues to hope for the same luck on New Year's Eve, as he returns annually on the most crowded day of the year to celebrate his birthday.

Gavin is the editor of DisneyDose.com, a website that focuses on educating Disney fans through exclusive interviews, breaking news updates, and photos from Disneyland. The site has received numerous features in outlets including *Forbes*, the Huffington Post, Buzzfeed, the *Los Angeles Times*, and many others.

He is also the host of the Disney Dose podcast, where new interviews with Disney Imagineers and others who helped create the magic are shared frequently.

In 2014, Gavin founded MickeyVisit.com, the ultimate online planning resource for Disneyland.

Do you have a secret or story from Disneyland to share? Write gavin@disneydose.com.

About the Publisher

Theme Park Press is the largest independent publisher of Disney and Disney-related pop culture books in the world.

Established in November 2012 by Bob McLain, Theme Park Press has released best-selling print and digital books about such topics as Disney films and animation, the Disney theme parks, Disney historical and cultural studies, park touring guides, autobiographies, fiction, and more.

Theme Park Press authors and contributors are a Disney who's who, ranging from well-known Disney historians and commentators like Jim Korkis, Sam Gennawey, and Didier Ghez, to Disney notables and legends like Floyd Norman, Bill "Sully" Sullivan, Rolly Crump, and Bob Gurr.

For our complete catalog and a list of forthcoming titles, please visit:

ThemeParkPress.com

or contact the publisher at:

bob@themeparkpress.com

Theme Park Press Newsletter

For a free, occasional email newsletter to keep you posted on new book releases, new author signings, and other events, as well as contests and exclusive excerpts and supplemental content, send email to:

theband@themeparkpress.com

or sign up at:

ThemeParkPress.com

More Books from Theme Park Press

Theme Park Press publishes dozens of books each year for Disney fans and for general and academic audiences. Here are just a few of our titles. For the complete catalog, including book descriptions and excerpts, please visit:

ThemeParkPress.com

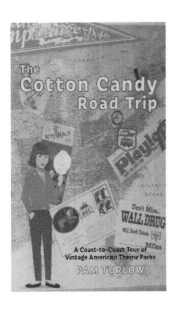

The Cotton Candy Road Trip

A Coast-to-Coast Tour of Vintage American Theme Parks

PAM TURLOW

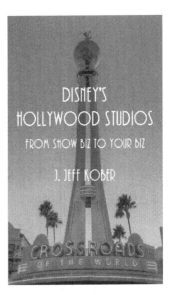

DISNEY'S HOLLYWOOD STUDIOS

FROM SHOW BIZ TO YOUR BIZ

J. JEFF KOBER

CROSSROADS
OF THE WORLD

Disney Melodies

Karl Beaudry   The Magic of Disney Music

"Prepare to be enchanted, bewildered and mesmerized by this   Guillermo del Toro
beat-by-beat account of the Haunted Mansion's creation."   Award-winning film director

The Unauthorized Story of
Walt Disney's
Haunted Mansion

Jeff Baham

Foreword by Rolly Crump

Who's the Leader of the Club?

Walt Disney's Leadership Lessons

JIM KORKIS

Foreword by Henry Hardt
Professor of Business Law and Professor of Finance
Buena Vista University

MURDER

IN THE MAGIC KINGDOM

Annie Salisbury

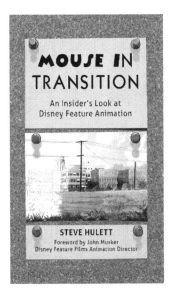

MOUSE IN TRANSITION

An Insider's Look at
Disney Feature Animation

STEVE HULETT

Foreword by John Musker
Disney Feature Films Animation Director

Walt Disney

AND THE PROMISE OF

Progress City

SAM GENNAWEY

Foreword by Werner Weiss

THE
RIDE DELEGATE
Memoir of a Walt Disney World VIP Tour Guide

Annie Salisbury

SERVICE
With
CHARACTER
The Disney Studio & World War II
by David Lesjak

Sara
EARNS HER EARS

My Secret Walt Disney World
Cast Member Diary

SARA LOPES
Earning Your Ears: Volume Three

THE
VAULT OF WALT
VOLUME 3
Even More Unofficial Disney Stories Never Told

Jim Korkis

Made in the USA
Lexington, KY
12 June 2016